D1283746

TV Station

By Jennifer Colby

CHERRY LAKE
Publishing

Published in the United States of America by
Cherry Lake Publishing
Ann Arbor, Michigan
www.cherrylakepublishing.com

Content Adviser: Nathan Southern
Reading Adviser: Marla Conn MS, Ed., Literacy specialist, Read-Ability, Inc.

Photo Credits: © Olena Yakobchuk/Shutterstock Images, cover, 1; © Monkey Business Images/
Shutterstock Images, 4, 14; ©DeshaCAM/Shutterstock Images, 6; © eldar nurkovic/
Shutterstock Images, 8; © Phillip Holland/Shutterstock Images, 10; © kldy/
Shutterstock Images, 12; © Stock image/Shutterstock Images, 16; © Blend Images/
Shutterstock Images, 18; © michaeljung/Shutterstock Images, 20

Library of Congress Cataloging-in-Publication Data
Names: Colby, Jennifer, 1971- author.
Title: TV station / by Jennifer Colby.
Description: Ann Arbor : Cherry Lake Publishing, 2016. | Series: 21st century
  junior library ; 1 | Includes bibliographical references and index.
Identifiers: LCCN 2015048514| ISBN 9781634710794 (hardcover) | ISBN 9781634711784 (pdf) |
ISBN 9781634712774 (pbk.) | ISBN 9781634713764 (ebook)
Subjects: LCSH: Television—Vocational guidance—United States—Juvenile
  literature.
Classification: LCC PN1992.55 .C55 2016 | DDC 384.5506/502373—dc23
LC record available at http://lccn.loc.gov/2015048514

Cherry Lake Publishing would like to acknowledge the work of The Partnership for 21st Century Learning.
Please visit www.p21.org for more information.

Printed in the United States of America
Corporate Graphics

CONTENTS

Do you enjoy watching TV with your family?

What Is a TV Station?

What will the weather be like today? What is happening in your town? You can turn on a TV news show to find out. A TV station makes the news show. Many people work at a TV station. TV is short for television.

News shows are recorded on sets in a TV station.

Most TV shows are **broadcast** from TV stations. They are **recorded** by cameras and shown later. News shows are live. They are happening as you watch them. The people on TV are talking at the same time you hear them.

Think!

Think about the TV shows you watch. What do you learn from them? Do you think they are live? Do you think they were recorded?

Directors need to make important choices.

TV Station Workers

Many people work at a TV station. You do not see all of them on your screen. The most important person you do not see is the **director**. The director decides how each show is put together. The director decides what you see on your screen.

Videographers use cameras to record and broadcast events on TV.

Who else works at a TV station?

The **producer** asks guests to be on a show. The producer also decides what stories to **cover**. **Reporters** talk about news stories. **Videographers** record those stories and local events. Many things happen all around. People want to know about them. People want to see these events on TV.

Ask Questions!

Do you know any reporters? Ask them about the stories they work on. Where do they work? Do they need to travel? What types of stories do they work on?

TV station helicopters record the news events that you watch on TV.

Some TV station workers drive vans full of **equipment**. Others fly **helicopters!** They help reporters and videographers get to news events. They carry cameras, microphones, and other equipment.

People work together to present news stories.

Writers write the news stories. They make sure the stories are correct.

Editors put film together to make a story. They need to fit the stories into the right amount of time. News **anchors** are in front of the cameras. They read the stories.

Create!

What is happening in your neighborhood? Write a news story about it! Get together with your friends. Record a news show! Who will be the news anchors? Who will be the videographer? Who will be the director?

Technicians make sure the sound and lights work.

There are other workers at a TV station. **Meteorologists** report on the weather. Other reporters talk about sports and traffic. **Technicians** run the sound and the lights. **Graphic designers** and **photographers** create the images you see on the screen.

Look!

Watch the images on news stories. Are they photos, drawings, charts, or words? Do the images make the news more interesting? Do they help you understand the story?

Make your own TV news show with your friends.

Do You Want to Work at a TV Station?

There are many different jobs at a TV station. Are you interested in working at one? You can get ready now! Practice your writing skills. Practice talking in front of other people. Learn more about cameras and recording equipment.

You could be in front of a TV camera.

Would you like to visit a TV station? Ask if you can take a tour. See what each worker does. Notice how workers solve problems. How do they work with each other? Do you want to be part of the action?

Make a Guess!

Is there a TV station near your town? How many people work at it? Go to the local TV station's Web site to see if you can find out. You may be surprised by how many people work there.

GLOSSARY

anchors (ANG-kurz) people who read the news on a TV show

broadcast (BRAWD-kast) sent out through TV or radio

cover (KUHV-ur) to report news about an event

director (duh-REK-tur) the person who is in charge of a TV show

editors (ED-ih-turz) people who put film together to make a news story

equipment (ih-KWIP-muhnt) supplies or tools needed for a special purpose

graphic designers (GRAF-ik dih-ZINE-urz) people who create maps, charts, drawings, and other illustrations

helicopters (HEL-ih-kop-turz) aircraft with large, rotating blades on top and no wings

meteorologists (mee-tee-uh-RAH-luh-jists) experts on the weather

photographers (fuh-TAH-gruh-furz) people who take photographs as a job

producer (pruh-DOOS-ur) a person who decides what will be covered on a TV show

recorded (rih-KORD-id) to store sounds and images so that they can be heard and seen later

reporters (rih-PORT-urz) people who gather and report the news

technicians (tek-NISH-uhnz) people who work with specialized equipment

videographers (vid-ee-OG-ruh-furz) people who record sounds and pictures on video

FIND OUT MORE

BOOKS

Spilsbury, Louise, and Richard Spilsbury. *The Television*. North Mankato, MN: Heinemann-Raintree, 2012.

Weil, Jamie. *Asking Questions about What's on Television*. Ann Arbor, MI: Cherry Lake Publishing, 2015.

WEB SITES

ETV Commission—Kids Work! Inside the TV Station
http://knowitall.org/kidswork/etv/index.html
A virtual workplace designed to give students an interactive experience.

The News Kids
http://thenewskids.org/
Watch news programs by kid journalists as they explore the world by developing and employing the skills of television journalists.

INDEX

A
anchors, 15

B
broadcasts, 7

C
cameras, 7, 13, 15, 19

D
directors, 9, 15

E
editors, 15
equipment, 13, 19

G
graphic designers, 17
guests, 11

H
helicopters, 13

L
lights, 17
live shows, 7

M
meteorologists, 17
microphones, 13

P
photographers, 17
practice, 15, 19
producers, 11

R
recordings, 7, 11, 15, 19
reporters, 11, 13, 17

S
sound, 17
sports, 17
stories, 11, 15, 17

T
technicians, 17
television, 5, 7, 11
traffic, 17

V
vans, 13
videographers, 11, 13, 15

W
weather, 5, 17
Web sites, 21
workers, 9, 11, 13, 15, 17, 21
writers, 15

ABOUT THE AUTHOR

Jennifer Colby is the author of many books for children. She is a high school librarian in Michigan. She was on a news show in college when a local TV station interviewed her.

24